ב״ה
OCT. 13

DEAREST MOTHER & FATHER,

THANK YOU FOR
SHOWERING ME WITH YOUR
LOVE, LAUGHTER, POSSESSIONS,
ENERGY, KINDNESS, TIME,
WISDOM, AND .... SO
MUCH MORE. I'M THE
MOST FORTUNATE DAUGHTER.
MAY THE MASTER OF THE
UNIVERSE CONTINUE TO
FLOOD US WITH SIMCHAS,
MAZEL, FINE HEALTH,
PEACE, AND KINDNESS.
Love,
Your Daughter

MIND SHOWER

a sensitive nature diary by Chikara Amano

MIND SHOWER

a sensitive nature diary by Chikara Amano

マインドシャワー／天野主税作品集

| Smiling Chinese milk vetch

| A milky haze above the Azusa River

A pretty robin beside a waterfall

The echo of cymbals in the misty morning

| A lonely magtail in a golden ring

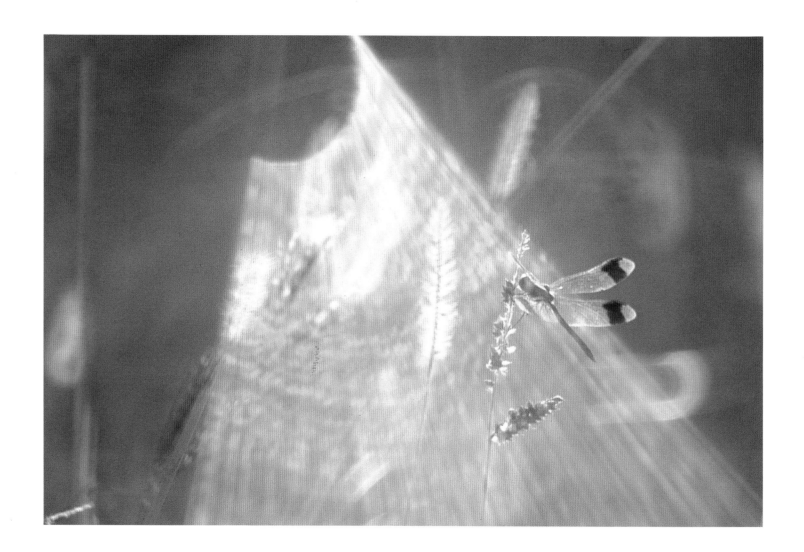

Comfortable snow cushions
Three runaways in the forest (P. 28-29)

| A rambler in the bush

| Chorus in green grass

Glove flower garden in full bloom | 37

A fast swimmer in clear water

Torrent of a flooded river

A Japanese wag amidst the sound of water | 41

| A bird playing a bright melody

| Memory of summer

Young leaves in a fresh morning
A tree calling summer clouds (P. 58-59)

| Hillside with a lonely cloud

| Boisterous dance of sea gulls

| A lake in summer morning light

| Twilight-tinted lake

Message／Chikara Amano

以前、ヨーロッパを旅して、ウイーンの森にある公園のベンチに腰かけていた時、数羽の
シジュウカラがすぐ近くに寄ってきて、ぼくの肩に止まったのです。

日本ではまずありえないことなので驚いたのですが、偶然もっていたピーナッツをポケッ
トから取り出し、掌にくだいてのせると、鳥たちは何のためらいもなく、かわるがわる餌
台となったぼくの手からピーナッツをついばんでくれたのです。

その時の掌に伝わる彼等の温い感触はたとえることのできない快感として現在でも忘れる
ことはできません。

鳥を撮ることからスタートしたぼくの写真は、その時の延長でありウイーンの森での夢よ
再びなのかもしれません。都市から自然へとその温もりを求めて旅から旅へ……。

ぼくの出会う野生の鳥や動物たち、あるいは自然は、ヨーロッパで出会った鳥たちのよう
に簡単にコミュニケートしてくれません。

彼らは危険を感じるぼくからはつねに安全距離を保って行動します。

その野生たちと自分との距離を縮めるのはレンズを変えるだけではどうしようもなく、鳥や
動物たちに限らず、花や虫、一滴の朝露、一本の草や葉など、自然を形成するすべてに対し
て、彼らを見つめる心の距離を短縮する以外に方法がないのではないかと思っているのです。

近づくこと、つまり生命が集ってきた自然との距離を暖めあうことができるのは惚れる、
一瞬でもいいから対象を愛し、ハートフルにバイヴレーションを交感するということでは
ないでしょうか。結果として人とのつきあいと同じだと気がついたのです。

そんなことをつねづね考えながらファインダーを覗いているのですが、はたしてこの写真集
を手にして下さる方々と、ぼくとの心の距離は少しでも暖めあうことができるでしょうか？
ジョン・レノンがぼくらに『イマジン』をプレゼントしてくれたように……。

最後にこの写真集を作るにあたって、IPCの中川右介氏、デザイナーの岡本明氏、オリオン
プレスの高田光夫氏の三氏には特にお世話になりました。この場をおかりして感謝、お礼
申し上げます。

I traveled to Europe and had a good time in Vienna. When I was sitting on a bench in the park, some titmice came near to me and one of them alighted on my shoulder. This could never happen in Japan, so I was very surprised. I took some peanuts out of my pocket and put them on my hand. Then they settled on my hand and began to peck at them without hesitation. There was still a warm feeling left in my hand after they flied away.

A few years ago, I started to take pictures of birds and since then, I have been looking for all the warm things composing nature. I came across various kinds of wild birds, animals and plants in Japan, but they never easily communicated with me. Since human beings are dangerous to them, they keep their distance from me. The telephoto lens can be of some use for shortening the distance between the object and me, but not sufficient for close commuication with nature.

The only way to commmunicate with nature, composed as it is, of innumerable lives, is to fall in love with and talk with nature itself. It works the same as human relations. When I look into the viewfinder, I always keep it in mind.

So I hope you and I can communicate with each other through my images in "Mind Shower" just as John Lennon did in "IMAGINE".

Last but not least , I would like to thank the following people for their help with the publication : Mr. Yusuke Nakagawa of IPC, designer Mr. Akira Okamoto and Mr. Mitsuo Takada of Orion Press.

Information

マインドシャワー／天野主税作品集

著者／天野主税
装幀・デザイン／岡本　明
企画・編集／高田光夫(オリオンプレス)
発行人／中川右介
発行所／株式会社アイピーシー(**IPC**)
　　　　〒171東京都豊島区西池袋3-30-10すやまビル
　　　　TEL.03-3980-7010 FAX.03-3980-7533

　　　　振替 東京8-118094
印刷・製本／株式会社耕文社
第一版 第一刷発行／1989年10月30日　第三刷発行／1991年4月30日
定価はカバーに表示してあります。
乱丁・落丁はお取り替えします。
写真及び記事の無断転載を禁じます。

MIND SHOWER

a sensitive nature diary —— photographed by Chikara Amano

Publisher／Yusuke Nakagawa
Editor／Mitsuo Takada
Designer／Akira Okamoto
Published by **INTER PRESS CORPORATION** （**IPC**）
Nishi-Ikebukuro 3-30-10, Toshima-ku, Tokyo, 171, JAPAN

Printed in Japan